RAND

# Response to the National Research Council's Assessment of RAND's *Controlling Cocaine* Study

Drug Policy Research Center
Jonathan P. Caulkins

*With*
James Chiesa,
Susan S. Everingham

A 1994 RAND study, *Controlling Cocaine: Supply Versus Demand Programs* (Rydell and Everingham), drew widely cited conclusions regarding the relative cost-effectiveness of spending additional drug control moneys on treatment and various modes of enforcement. A National Research Council (NRC) committee last year issued a critique of that report concluding that it was not a good basis for policymaking.

Modeling is an inexact science, and there is plenty of room for experts to disagree on methods and conclusions. We feel, however, that the NRC's critique warrants a reply, for two reasons. First, it appears to rest on incomplete information regarding the RAND model. Our differences with the assessment are thus not simply a matter of varying judgment or opinion. Second, the critique was issued by a distinguished panel at the request of the Office of National Drug Control Policy. Barring objection, we fear that many in the drug policy community may tend to accept the conclusions of the panel as the last word on this topic.

This document presents a detailed point-by-point response to the NRC panel's critique. It was prepared by Jonathan Caulkins with substantial input from James Chiesa and Susan Everingham. The reviewers were David Boyum and Peter Reuter, to whom we are all grateful for numerous comments that resulted in improvements to the text.

We summarize the NRC panel's criticisms (in italics) and our responses here.

- *The RAND study assumes that the unit price of supplying cocaine decreases with the total quantity of cocaine supplied, whereas for conventional goods the usual assumption is of price increasing with quantity supplied. This could influence the study's conclusions about the effectiveness of enforcement policies.*

  Although we stand behind the price-quantity relationship assumed in *Controlling Cocaine,* we did reprogram the model to include the panel's alternative assumption, and the results are substantially the same.

- *The RAND model uses cocaine seizures as the primary measure of supply control activity, when they alone may not accurately reflect that activity.*

  Actually, the model considers asset seizure, arrests, imprisonment, and incarceration of cocaine-using sellers, although these are assumed to be proportional to product seizures. Rewriting the equations in terms of one of the other supply control effects would not change the results. The approach currently taken is consistent with a desire to test the effects of expanding average practice within each category of enforcement strategies; this approach is parallel to that taken in the report's analysis of treatment.

- *The RAND study ignores the nonmonetary costs of dealer imprisonment (e.g., stigma).*

  The model assumes that the price a dealer charges covers all costs and risks, monetary and nonmonetary (or the dealer would find some other line of work).

- *Subsequent research suggests that cocaine consumers respond to price changes more dramatically than assumed in the model, so the study may underestimate the cost-effectiveness of enforcement.*

  When better estimates of this parameter became available, RAND published revised estimates based on those newer figures (see Caulkins et al., 1997). They reduce treatment's edge vis-a-vis enforcement, but by no means reverse it, and they do not affect the relative estimates among the three enforcement programs.

- *The RAND model uses a single parameter to describe a variety of possible responses of cocaine consumers to price changes.*

  Actually, the model uses seven such parameters to cover different intensities of use and transitions between different use states.

Some of the NRC panel's criticisms are valid. It is true, as the committee says, that the model's estimate of treatment's effectiveness relies on very limited data and that the model has not been validated against other data. However, no better treatment data or data suitable for validation were then available. Nor is it clear that any have yet surfaced. More to the point, more-reliable data would influence the qualitative conclusions only if they show treatment to be less cost-effective than assumed in *Controlling Cocaine*. In this context, it is worth pointing out that the study has been criticized in other quarters for *under*estimating treatment's effectiveness.

It is also true that the model assumes, as was the norm when the study was done, that cost increases at one point in the cocaine supply chain cause merely additive increases down the chain; that is, a doubling of the price at one point does not, in the model, cause a doubling down the line. Recognizing the importance of this assumption, RAND led efforts to test it. The results were inconclusive but suggested that multiplicative increases may pertain over some portions of the distribution chain. RAND subsequently published a qualitative analysis of this issue and proposed further quantitative research (unfortunately not funded to date).

We would add to the concerns raised by the panel the need—noted in the original study—to refine the characterization of drug user careers and the need to update the study. Indeed, RAND has always viewed *Controlling Cocaine* as a path-breaking study—a first, not a final, attempt to apply systems modeling to drug policy issues. Thus, in a fundamental sense we agree with the panel: Further work is needed to improve the objective basis for drug policymaking. Such an improvement constitutes the broader mission of the NRC panel.

Meanwhile, current policies are sustained, new ones introduced. We believe policy should be informed by the best methods and information available—that considering the results of analysis representing the current state of the art, imperfect though that might be, is better than relying on no analysis. Policymaking cannot afford to let "better" become the enemy of "good enough." Improvements in data and methods are always being made, so the state of the art will never be unencumbered by weaknesses. Nonetheless, we would share the NRC panel's hesitancy to rely on *Controlling Cocaine* for policy formation if the model fell short of what is achievable under the current state of the art. As indicated above, we do not believe that is the case. We thus urge continued reliance on the policy implications drawn from this evolving model until further work pushes the state of the art beyond it.

Audrey Burnam and Martin Iguchi<br>
Codirectors, Drug Policy Research Center

# CONTENTS

# FIGURE

# TABLES

# INTRODUCTION

Last year, the National Research Council's Committee for Data and Research for Policy on Illegal Drugs issued its *Assessment of Two Cost-Effectiveness Studies on Cocaine Control Policy* (Manski, Pepper, and Thomas, 1999; cited hereafter as "NRC report"). One of the studies evaluated was *Controlling Cocaine: Supply Versus Demand Programs* (Rydell and Everingham, 1994; cited hereafter as *Controlling Cocaine* or *CC*), issued by RAND's Drug Policy Research Center (DPRC). According to the committee,

> The study documents a significant effort to identify and model important elements of the market for cocaine. It represents a serious attempt to formally characterize the complex interaction of producers and users and the subtle process through which alternative cocaine control policies may affect consumption and prices [p. 1].

The committee also stated, however,

> The study makes many unsubstantiated assumptions about the process through which cocaine is produced, distributed, and consumed. Plausible changes in these assumptions can change not only the quantitative findings reported, but also the main qualitative conclusions of the study. Hence the study's findings do not constitute a persuasive basis for the formation of cocaine control policy [p. 2].

The reasons the committee gives for the latter conclusion indicate that it is based on insufficient information and, in some respects, an incomplete analysis of the information available. This attachment responds point by point to the "committee's main concerns" about the *Controlling Cocaine* report, as described on pages 15–28 of the NRC report.

# ESTIMATES OF EFFECTS OF DRUG TREATMENT PROGRAMS ON COCAINE USE

The NRC report observes, "The RAND study bases its estimates of treatment effectiveness on the Treatment Outcome Prospective Study (TOPS)" (p. 16). According to the NRC committee, "TOPS focused largely on treatment effectiveness for heroin users." For this and other reasons, the committee finds it "not clear that the TOPS data provide information relevant to the evaluation of current treatment programs for heavy cocaine users." Aside from the limitations in the data themselves, the committee worries that "the RAND interpretation of the data may make treatment programs seem more or less cost-effective than they actually are" (p. 17). In particular, the committee is concerned that RAND inferred real treatment effects where none may exist (p. 19). The committee is disturbed that RAND reported the sensitivity of its findings to posttreatment effectiveness but not to in-treatment effectiveness.

First, let us address the focus of TOPS. Among residential treatment clients included in the TOPS data, the proportions that were regular heroin and cocaine users one year before entering treatment were similar; among outpatient drug-free treatment clients, more had been regular cocaine users a year prior to treatment than had been regular heroin users (Hubbard et al., 1989, p. 180). Only among outpatient methadone clients did regular heroin users outnumber regular cocaine users, who nonetheless made up nearly 30 percent of the total. More important, the *Controlling Cocaine* study used treatment data only for regular cocaine users in residential and outpatient drug-free treatment; data for non–cocaine users in these modalities and data for outpatient methadone clients were not used.

With respect to the remainder of the NRC's critique of the data and their interpretation, it is certainly true that, at the time of the *Controlling Cocaine* study, available treatment effectiveness data fell well short of the ideal for support of cost-effectiveness analysis—and they still do. Selection bias has been a problem both in large-scale, uncontrolled studies like TOPS and in small-scale random-assignment studies, where the populations and programs are not representative of the universe of treatment, which is what *CC* sought to model. *CC*'s authors estimated the necessary parameters based on their reading of the literature and conversations with treatment experts. Of course, they knew and worried about the "fundamental problems that arise in attempting to infer treatment effects from observational data on treatment outcomes in heterogeneous populations" (NRC report, p. 18). However, in their judgment, any resulting overestimates of effectiveness were offset by the various conservative features of the analysis. For example, they put two-thirds of their nominal posttreatment "abstainers" into the light-use pool from which users could relapse; only one-third actually became abstinent in the model. Moreover, they chose as their principal outcome measure the quantity of consumption averted, rather than such other policy-relevant measures as drug-related spending or crime. (Whatever treatment's cost-effectiveness relative to price-raising enforcement at reducing consumption, it is almost certainly more cost-effective with respect to controlling drug-related spending and hence drug-related crime, as is argued in *CC* Chapter Five.) *CC* followed Hubbard et al. in taking those in treatment three months or less as the control group. This sacrificed any benefits realized by that group and depressed the treatment-vs.-control difference from what it would have been with a no-treatment control. Finally, *CC*'s authors did not account for the possibility that drug users in treatment might, through persuasion or example, induce other users to reduce consumption. These aspects of the analysis all have the effect of pushing the treatment results to the conservative side. Indeed, we have as often been told that *CC*'s treatment estimates are too small as that they are too large.

Thus, it is possible, as the committee states, that RAND's interpretation of the data may have made treatment seem either more or less cost-effective than it actually is. This is the inevitable consequence of uncertainty. It does not seem, however, that it would have been useful, as the committee believes (p. 19), for the *CC* authors to have extended their sensitivity analysis to encompass a zero effectiveness for treatment. The hypothesis that treatment may benefit no one is at odds with a variety of other assessments (e.g., Institute of Medicine, 1996).

In retrospect, reporting an explicit sensitivity analysis relating to in-treatment effectiveness would have been desirable. Such an analysis was actually performed, but the *CC* authors did not feel the results were interesting enough to report. In the course of writing this document, we reproduced the two-dimensional sensitivity analysis and confirmed that uncertainty about posttreatment effects is of substantially greater import than is uncertainty about in-treatment effects. (The *CC* authors performed many sensitivity analyses. In the interests of space, they reported only results for the parameters to which the conclusions were most sensitive.)

The uncertainty surrounding the results can be recognized by explicitly limiting the applicability of the study's results to treatment programs with the parameters assumed—an in-treatment effectiveness of 79 percent and a posttreatment effectiveness of 13 percent. Indeed, when citing the results of the study, RAND has typically been careful to include these parameters.

Notwithstanding the matter of which treatment parameters are correct, *CC*'s authors clearly succeeded in showing that

- even if treatment programs' posttreatment effects are as low as 13 percent, they are highly cost-effective (in absolute terms, quite apart from any comparison with other drug control strategies)

- uncertainty in treatment relapse and effectiveness rates accounts for much of the uncertainty in the relative cost-effectiveness of treatment and enforcement, so estimating these rates with more confidence is an important research task.

## MODELING THE SUPPLY OF COCAINE

### Shape of the Average Cost Curve

This criticism comes in multiple parts, but the essence is that "Inferences on the effects of supply-control policies depend critically on the assumed shape of the average cost curve" (p. 19). That statement is true only in the narrow sense that the specific numerical estimates depend on the shape; as demonstrated below, the basic qualitative conclusions do not. The panel describes its concerns as pertaining to three of *CC*'s assumptions, as follows.

*Price Equals Average Cost:* The *CC* model assumes that high monetary profits are compensation for the various risks of the trade, i.e., it adopts the "risks and prices" paradigm (Reuter and Kleiman, 1986). The committee asserts, "If, on the contrary, some profits are economic rents that more than compensate for costs and risks, then the industry average [cost] curve will be upward sloping (see, e.g., Bresnahan, 1989)" (p. 20). To test this assertion, we changed the model to include economic rents,[1] and the effects were minimal. In particular, we made economic rents equal to a fixed proportion (denoted *er* in Table 1) of the costs of asset seizures, arrest, and incarceration compensation at a given level (source zone, transit zone, or within the United States).[2] This did not make the supply curve slope upward (note all supply elasticities in the table are negative) or have much influence on the cost-effectiveness estimates.[3]

We experimented with other variants of economic rents that had somewhat larger effects. In particular, one can create a variant of Boyum's (1992) "investment model" by making other assumptions about the nature of economic rents. As Boyum argued in his thesis, this is one way to generate a "multiplicative model" of price transmission (this variant is discussed further below, under "Supply Control Policies and Average Production Costs").

On a theoretical basis, it is curious that the NRC committee would find "no compelling case" for price equating to average cost, i.e., that profits and rents are zero. It is common practice in economics to assume zero profit unless there is substantial evidence to the contrary—evidence which in the case of the cocaine market is thin at best. Accounting profits are certainly large, but economic profits not necessarily so (see, e.g., Reuter, MacCoun, and Murphy, 1990). Boyum (1992) has even argued that economic rents may be negative for drug sellers.

It is also unclear why, as the NRC report claims, economic rents necessarily imply an upward-sloping supply curve. (Incidentally, the

Table 1

*CC* Model Estimates of Cost-Effectiveness, Accounting for Economic Rents

| | $er = 0$ | $er = 0.1$ | $er = 0.2$ | $er = 0.4$ |
|---|---|---|---|---|
| Cost-effectiveness[a] | | | | |
| Source country control | 783 | 785 | 787 | 790 |
| Interdiction | 366 | 368 | 369 | 372 |
| Domestic enforcement | 246 | 243 | 241 | 236 |
| Treatment | 34 | 33 | 33 | 33 |
| Ratio (domestic enforcement:treatment) | 7.3 | 7.3 | 7.3 | 7.2 |
| Supply elasticity | −3.6 | −3.5 | −3.4 | −3.2 |

[a]Cost (in millions of 1992 dollars) of reducing modeled U.S. cocaine consumption by 1 percent.

NOTE: Larger numbers indicate smaller cost-effectiveness.

Bresnahan article does not appear to us to support this claim.) Supernormal profits per kilogram sold could be increasing or decreasing in the size of the market. In particular, inasmuch as a "thin" market makes it easier to extract monopoly rents (because it is harder for customers at all levels to shop around), rents could decrease as market volume expands.

***Constant Marginal Cost:*** The NRC report asserts, "If there are resource constraints relevant to the production of cocaine, the cocaine average cost curve slopes upward, if all else is equal" (p. 20). (From the context, the panel apparently intends to include distribution within "production"; we do the same here, as did *CC*.) Actually, there is little evidence that conventional factors of cocaine production are meaningfully constrained in the long run.[4] But even if they were, this turns out to have very modest effects on the estimates of the cost-effectiveness of the supply control programs.

We have rerun the model with production costs made convex in the amount produced, i.e., assuming that marginal cost increases with quantity. The convexity of the curve is governed by a new parameter $dd$.[5]

If $dd = 1$, the model reduces to the original *CC* model. Table 2 gives the sensitivity of the cost-effectiveness results to the parameter $dd$, up to $dd = 4$ (the value used in Figure 2 in the NRC report; see p. 48, where the parameter is called $d$).

The table shows that the cost-effectiveness of enforcement is not very sensitive to the assumption about the convexity of production costs. The parameter has a stronger effect on the cost-effectiveness of treatment because, if the supply curve has a negative slope, treatment's downward pressure on demand causes prices to rise and thus further decreases consumption. If the supply curve has a positive slope, this "market multiplier" effect (see Caulkins et al., 1999) disappears.[6]

***Supply Control Policies Impose Fixed Costs:*** The committee notes,

> In the RAND model, industry average cost declines as a consequence of an unsubstantiated assumption about the effects of supply-control policies. Such policies are assumed to generate seizures that increase less, proportionally, than output [p. 20].

**Table 2**

**CC Model Estimates of Cost-Effectiveness, Allowing for a Convex Cost Curve**

|  | $dd = 1$ | $dd = 2$ | $dd = 3$ | $dd = 4$ |
|---|---|---|---|---|
| Cost-effectiveness[a] |  |  |  |  |
| Source country control | 783 | 795 | 788 | 772 |
| Interdiction | 366 | 364 | 362 | 361 |
| Domestic enforcement | 246 | 238 | 233 | 231 |
| Treatment | 34 | 42 | 51 | 60 |
| Ratio (domestic enforcement:treatment) | 7.2 | 5.7 | 4.6 | 3.8 |
| Supply elasticity | −3.56 | 5.85 | 1.45 | 0.78 |

[a]Cost (in millions of 1992 dollars) of reducing U.S. cocaine consumption by 1 percent.

NOTE: Larger numbers indicate smaller cost-effectiveness.

In fact, the assumption about cocaine seizures is only part of the reason why price falls with quantity supplied in the *CC* model. Much of the declining average cost comes from, in Kleiman's (1993) terms, "enforcement swamping." That is, a bigger market swamps enforcement resources and reduces unit price, and, conversely, a smaller market focuses enforcement resources and places a bigger enforcement "tax" on the product. Cocaine seizures are only one aspect of the "tax" imposed through enforcement. Compensation for the risks of arrest, asset seizure, and incarceration is also present and important in the *CC* model. Such compensation also contributes to the downward slope.

But given that cocaine seizures are indeed a factor, there are two issues. First, is *CC* likely to be wrong in assuming that the quantity seized with a given level of enforcement spending increases less, proportionally, than production increases? Second, does it make a big difference to the results?

With respect to the first issue, the *CC* assumption is equivalent to saying that, for a given level of enforcement spending, the quantity of cocaine seized makes up a decreasing fraction of production as production increases. (Again, "production" here refers to the output of a given stage in the cocaine pipeline, e.g., shipments from the source country.) The expression of this assumption within the *CC* model, which can be obtained algebraically from Equation B.9 on *CC* p. 64, is

$$f \ = \ X/G = ZX/[pWG^* + (1-p)WG]$$

where  $f$  =  fraction of cocaine production seized,
       $X$  =  quantity of cocaine seized,
       $G$  =  production in the current (modeled) year,
       $Z$  =  cost to the government of seizing drugs per kilogram seized,
       $p$  =  parameter governing how seizure costs depend on market volume,
       $W$  =  average seizure cost per unit seized in reference year (1992), and
       $G^*$ =  production in the reference year.

The details of this relationship are not of concern here. It is clear, however, that for constant expenditures on seizures ($ZX$), as production ($G$) increases, the fraction seized ($f$) decreases. Let's state this relationship in terms of cost. Multiplying through by the right-side denominator and expressing $X$ as $fG$ gives

$$ZfG \ = \ (1-p)WfG + pWfG^*$$

or

$$\text{cost to seize a fraction } f \text{ of production} = (1-p)c_1G + pc_2,$$

where $c_1$ and $c_2$ are positive constants. Thus $CC$'s assumption, to which the committee objects, is that the cost of seizing a given fraction of shipments does not decrease with increasing amount shipped, and it is constant only if $p = 1$. Therefore, according to $CC$, it must cost at least as much in toto, for example, to seize a given proportion (say 25 percent) of production if production is 1,000 metric tons as it does if production is 500 metric tons. It is unclear how this assumption could be false, and the committee offers no explanation for how it could be.

With respect to the second issue, it turns out that the qualitative results do not depend critically on $CC$'s assumption regarding cocaine seizures and production levels. Table 3 shows the cost-effectiveness results when this assumption is varied. The first data column shows the base case results with $p = 0.5$. The second shows the results for

Table 3

**CC Model Estimates of Cost-Effectiveness, Allowing for Lower Seizure Costs
with Higher Quantities Produced**

|  | $p = 0.5$[a] | $p = 0.9$ | $p = 1.0$ | $p = 1.0$ $gg = 1.5$ | $p = 1.0$ $gg = 2.0$ |
|---|---|---|---|---|---|
| Cost-effectiveness[b] |  |  |  |  |  |
| Source country control | 783 | 761 | 754 | 720 | 672 |
| Interdiction | 366 | 364 | 363 | 360 | 357 |
| Domestic enforcement | 247 | 242 | 241 | 235 | 230 |
| Treatment | 34 | 36 | 37 | 41 | 47 |
| Ratio (domestic enforcement:treatment) | **7.3** | **6.7** | **6.5** | **5.7** | **4.9** |

[a]See text for explanation of column heads.

[b]Cost (in millions of 1992 dollars) of reducing U.S. cocaine consumption by 1 percent.

NOTE: Larger numbers indicate smaller cost-effectiveness.

$p = 0.9$, the upper end of the sensitivity range used in *CC*. When $p = 0.9$, the cost-effectiveness of enforcement improves by between 0.5 percent and 2.8 percent relative to when $p = 0.5$, depending on the type of enforcement. When $p$ is increased to 1.0, the cost of seizing a given fraction of production becomes independent of production quantity. That improves the cost-effectiveness of enforcement by another 0.5 percent to 0.9 percent, a trivial change (see the third data column in Table 3).

But the committee wanted to consider the possibility that the cost of seizing a given proportion of production might decrease as the quantity produced increases, so we modified the model to make

$$Z = W[(1-p) + p(G^*/G)^{gg}]$$

at each production stage, where $gg$ is a new parameter. When $p = 1$ and $gg > 1$, the cost of seizing a given fraction of production decreases as the quantity produced increases. For example, when $gg = 2$, it costs one-quarter as much to seize 25 percent of 500 metric tons as it does to seize 25 percent of 1,000 metric tons. As is clear from the last two columns of Table 3, the basic qualitative cost-effectiveness findings hold. The reason is that, as mentioned above, the *CC* model is not driven by seizures. Furthermore, most of the change in the ratio between enforcement and treatment comes not from the cost-effectiveness of enforcement but from that of treatment. (Incidentally, these changes do indeed generate an upward-sloping supply curve; the elasticity of supply for the last column in the table is +2.01. They just do not have much influence on the cost-effectiveness.)

***Varying Assumptions Together:***   The committee says, "Changes in any of the three RAND assumptions could easily generate an upward sloping market average cost curve for cocaine" (p. 20). This assertion is verified above for the second and third of the three assumptions, but in none of the cases does this change in supply curve slope affect the study's qualitative conclusions. What would happen, though, if more than one of the assumptions were varied simultaneously? We tried setting $er = 0.4$, $dd = 2$, and $p = 1.0$. We left $gg = 1$ because the committee provided no basis for $gg > 1$ and it is difficult to think of one. With those changes, the cost-effectiveness of source-country control improved by 2 percent, that of interdiction declined slightly, and that of domestic enforcement improved by 7.8 percent. The slope of the supply curve changed a lot (from an elasticity of –3.6 to an elasticity of +2.7). That reduced the cost-effectiveness of treatment by one-third, but treatment still retained an edge of more than 5:1 over the best enforcement program.

***NRC Report Appendix:***   The committee did not find it feasible to perform the reanalyses reported above. Instead, it undertook "to formulate and analyze a relatively simple model that expresses the main features of the RAND model" (p. 21). This model is presented in the appendix to the committee's report. It is used to generate a graph showing that the effect of increased cocaine seizures on cocaine consumption is greater with an upward-sloping supply curve than with a downward-sloping one.

Obviously, the lessons from the reanalyses reported here using the *CC* model itself supersede any obtained with an approximation to the model. The NRC model in particular is not a good approximation to the *CC* model and should not be used as a substitute. The NRC model is static, assumes supply cost does not vary with enforcement intensity, ignores the fact that cocaine market activities vary by zone (source, transition, domestic), and assumes that enforcement affects producer costs only through seizures. Anyone interested in the behavior of the *CC* model with different parameter values should run the *CC* model itself; the model is readily available and is not difficult to use.[7]

## Supply Control Policies and Average Production Costs

The committee observes that *CC* assumes price increases at one level (e.g., the source country) are passed on to lower levels (e.g., smuggling in the transition zone), in an "additive" rather than "multiplicative" fashion. That is, if price at the exit from one zone is $1 and at the exit from the next zone is $10, under the additive model a $1 price increase in the first zone will cause a $1 price increase in the next one (to $11); under the multiplicative model, the $1 price increase in the first zone represents a doubling that leads to a doubling of price in the next zone (to $20). The committee argues that it is unclear which model holds but that if the additive model does not hold, then *CC*, by assuming it does, would underestimate the effectiveness of source country control.

Although additive price transmission was the generally accepted model when the *CC* analysis was conducted in 1992–1993, an additive model is in fact a strong assumption (see Caulkins, 1994a,b).[8] However, in specifying the example given in the previous paragraph, the committee uses standard import price and coca base price. There is good reason for not extending the multiplicative argument back to coca base. The price data suggest that the multiplicative model does not hold that far up the distribution chain. If the multiplicative model holds and the upstream price varies substantially in percentage terms, one would expect to see a fairly strong correlation between the upstream and downstream prices. This is observed for cocaine prices within the United States between the kilogram-to-multikilogram levels and the retail level. It is not observed between coca base prices and downstream prices. (See the figure.)

## Seizures as a Measure of Supply-Control Activity

The committee asserts,

> The measure used to characterize the intensity of supply-control activities can influence findings of the cost-effectiveness of such activities. In the RAND study, the primary measure of supply-control activities—source country controls, interdiction, or do-

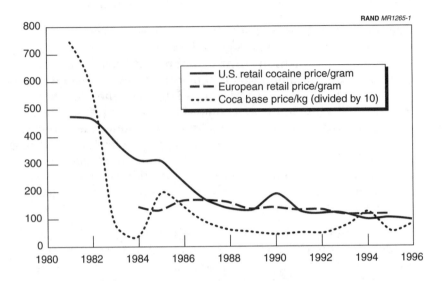

**Base and Retail Cocaine Prices Are Not Correlated**

mestic enforcement—is the amount of cocaine seized.  The study justifies use of this measure by asserting that seizures and supply-control activities are monotonically related and, hence, that seizures appropriately measure the intensity of supply-control activities . . . .

Seizures, however, may not actually measure the intensity of supply-control activities.  There are some policies that may successfully disrupt supply without seizing any cocaine whatsoever . . . [pp. 23–24].

The first half of this criticism is erroneous.  It is not true that cocaine seizures are the primary measure of supply control in *CC*.  *CC* characterizes enforcement activities by five direct effects—seizure of cocaine, seizure of assets, arrest sanctions, imprisonment sanctions, and incarceration of sellers who are also users—and one indirect effect (on production costs).  The direct effects are modeled as proportional to each other, so enforcement is no more characterized by cocaine seizures than it is by arrests or incarceration of sellers.  For expositional purposes, one is selected as the numeraire, but the choice is arbitrary. The equations can be rewritten with another numeraire with no effect whatsoever on the underlying calculations.

With respect to the second half of the NRC report's criticism, it is true that different enforcement tactics generate different mixes of enforcement "products" (e.g., more or fewer seizures per person incarcerated). Since *CC* makes no attempt to disaggregate different tactics within any production stage, it cannot model expansions in enforcement that alter the mix of tactics and, hence, the products of enforcement. That is a consequence of the model's focus on strategic options (domestic enforcement versus interdiction) not tactical choices (interdiction along one route versus another). It also reflects a simple, level-playing-field assumption about how budget increments are allocated. Since within any strategy some tactics are more cost-effective than others, every strategy can have a broad range of marginal cost-effectiveness outcomes depending on how wisely the increment is allocated. One could rig an analysis to make any given strategy beat another strategy by assuming that budget increments would go to the best tactics within the first strategy and the worst tactics within the second. To avoid such bias, *CC* assumes that all tactics currently employed by a strategy will be expanded proportionately. Of course, budgetary and bureaucratic realities can play out differently, but the *CC* approach has the advantages of being transparent and evenhanded.

## Nonprice Effects of Supply-Control Activities

The panel suggests that *CC* understates enforcement's effectiveness because

> [i]n illegal markets . . . both drug producers and consumers must reckon with important nonmonetary aspects of participation in the drug market. The relevant nonmonetary factors may include search costs and fear of stigma or imprisonment. The RAND study abstracts from these considerations and assumes that price movements suffice to equilibrate the market for cocaine. Yet, important supply control activities, particularly local law-enforcement, act primarily by raising the nonmonetary costs of participation in the drug market. In this respect, as in the others discussed above, the

RAND analysis may underestimate the cost-effectiveness of supply-control activities [p. 24].

The real question here is not whether RAND's analysis may underestimate supply control's cost-effectiveness but whether that underestimate is sufficient to vitiate the basic conclusions of the report. The committee does not offer a quantitative argument suggesting that it is. Following are some observations suggesting why *CC*'s conclusions should hold.

Again, the risks-and-prices paradigm gives monetary expression to certain nonmonetary effects. For example, in contrast to the committee's implication, the *CC* model does indeed account for fear of imprisonment on the part of producers. This fear is central to the risks-and-prices paradigm. Stigma effects are not considered explicitly. Inasmuch as stigma effects contributed to high prices in the base year of 1992, *CC* mistakenly credits those effects to one of the other components of the industry cost structure (e.g., conventional production costs or imprisonment costs). We have considered variations of *CC* that explicitly included stigma to see if it would substantially affect the results, and it does not.

Both stigma and economic factors could reduce drug availability, increasing "search times." Rocheleau and Boyum (1994) found that experienced heroin users spend about 35 minutes per $26 purchase. Therefore, even if users valued their time at $7/hour, search time would account for less than 15% of the combined cost to the user represented by purchase price and search time (Caulkins, 1998). It is not obvious why search times for cocaine in 1992 would be much greater than they were for the heroin users in Rocheleau and Boyum's study. Thus, it does not appear that there is much potential for increases in search time to have a large effect on the cost to users of making drug purchases.

But is it even likely that expanding enforcement activity would greatly affect these small search costs? We are skeptical it could for drugs in mature mass markets where consumption is dominated by heavy users (as was the case for cocaine in 1992). Riley (1997) finds that most cocaine and heroin users surveyed by the Drug Use Forecasting system reported that they knew of 10 to 20 suppliers of their drug of choice. Even if arresting one of a user's suppliers led to

100 additional hours of search time, which seems generous, the search time effects of retail enforcement would be an order of magnitude smaller than the "risks and prices" effects modeled in *CC* (again, see Caulkins, 1998, for elaboration of this discussion).[9]

## MODELING THE DEMAND FOR COCAINE

### The Price Elasticity of Demand

The committee notes,

> For some time, the conventional wisdom was that the demand for illegal substances is relatively price inelastic. Reflecting this belief, the RAND study chose a baseline value of –0.50 and performed a sensitivity analysis entertaining values between –0.38 and –0.75. Recent studies, however, suggest that the demand for cocaine may actually be much more price elastic, perhaps –1.0 or even more negative (see Caulkins, 1995; Grossman et al., 1996). If the price elasticity of demand is, in fact, less than –0.75, the RAND analysis understates the cost-effectiveness of supply-control activities [p. 26].

Obviously a 1994 report could not incorporate evidence from more recent studies, but it is a trivial matter to rerun the model with higher elasticity values. Indeed, RAND has already published updated estimates of the *CC* cost-effectiveness estimates using the newer, higher elasticity values (Caulkins et al., 1997, use a base case value of –1.0, with sensitivity analysis ranges of –0.5 to –1.5 or 0 to –2 depending on the specific analysis). Of course, the cost-effectiveness of supply control increases, but again, treatment retains a large advantage (4:1) over the strongest enforcement program considered in *CC*, and the rank order of the cost-effectiveness of the three enforcement programs is unchanged.

Also, note that the range of sensitivity values cited by the committee reflects only one aspect of *CC*'s sensitivity analysis. The *CC* report also included a breakeven chart (Figure F.2) that showed how high the elasticity of demand had to be for enforcement to become more cost-effective than treatment.

## The Complex Response of Cocaine Consumption to Prices

The committee states,

> The RAND demand model, with its single price elasticity of demand parameter, abstracts from much of the complexity of the behavior that determines cocaine use. . . . The RAND study assumes that light and heavy users of cocaine share the same sensitivity to price . . . . The addiction process may imply that price affects desistance from drug use differently than the way it affects initiation. The effects of price on initiation and intensification of drug use may be quite different as well. . . . For all of these reasons, it seems unlikely that a single price elasticity can adequately characterize how cocaine use responds to the price of cocaine [p. 26].

*CC* actually has seven demand elasticity parameters, representing elasticities of initiation, desistance from light use, escalation from light to heavy use, regression from heavy to light use, quitting heavy use, per-capita current consumption of light users, and per-capita current consumption of heavy users (see *CC*, Figure E.9). It is true that all seven elasticity parameters were varied in fixed proportions in *CC*'s sensitivity analysis. In 1992–93 there was almost no information in the literature concerning the relative magnitude of the components of the overall elasticity. Even today there isn't much empirical basis for determining their relative values. Thus, the *CC* model allocated the overall elasticity in a transparent way that is easy to describe. Specifically, the first five were $0.25e$ and the last two were $0.5e$, where $e$ was the overall (long-run) elasticity of demand. However, the fact that all seven were varied together in that analysis does not mean that they did not exist independently in the model.

It turns out that *CC*'s allocation does not seem to appreciably bias the results in treatment's favor. The total elasticity matters, so sensitivity analysis with respect to it is reported. *CC* does not report sensitivity analysis with respect to the relative magnitudes of the components of the overall elasticity. Table 4 reports recent runs of the *CC* model for the following scenarios:

1.  Make the five flow elasticities zero and double the short-term elasticities (keeping the overall long-term elasticity roughly the same).

2. Double the five flow elasticities and make the short-term elasticities zero (again keeping the overall long-term elasticity roughly the same).

3. Make short-term elasticities zero (thus reducing the overall elasticity of demand).

4. Cut the short-term elasticity of heavy-user consumption in half (again reducing the overall elasticity of demand).

In none of the four was the rank order of programs' cost-effectiveness changed. There are of course an arbitrarily large number of such scenarios that could be run. Each takes just a minute or two to create. Readers interested in elasticity partition effects should feel free to experiment with other scenarios.

The committee also remarks,

> Another simplification in the RAND model of the demand for cocaine is the absence of any consideration of cross-price elasticities with respect to other psychoactive substances . . . [U]nderstanding patterns of complementarity and substitution among drugs is essential to understanding the effects of control policy on drug use [pp. 26–27].[10]

### Table 4

### *CC* Model Estimates of Cost-Effectiveness, with Elasticity Components Varied

|  | Scenario[a] | | | |
|---|---|---|---|---|
|  | 1 | 2 | 3 | 4 |
| Cost-effectiveness[b] |  |  |  |  |
| Source country control | 742 | 867 | 1,864[c] | 998 |
| Interdiction | 347 | 405 | 869 | 465 |
| Domestic enforcement | 234 | 270 | 530 | 307 |
| Treatment | 32 | 35 | 37 | 35 |
| Supply elasticity | –3.56 | –3.56 | –3.56 | –3.56 |

[a]See text for scenario definition.

[b]Cost (in millions of 1992 dollars) of reducing U.S. cocaine consumption by 1 percent.

[c]Increases in funding of this magnitude are beyond the range for which extrapolations are valid.

NOTE: Larger numbers indicate smaller cost-effectiveness.

The committee's intent here is unclear. It may be pointing out the insufficiency of a model whose outcome measure is limited to cocaine consumption, when cocaine control strategies have implications for the use of other drugs. Or it may be faulting the *CC* model for not taking account of indirect effects on cocaine consumption mediated through the effects of cocaine control strategies on other drugs. For example, increasing the price of cocaine might drive cocaine users to drink more. That drinking might affect the rates at which light cocaine users escalate to heavy use, thereby affecting the demand for cocaine. Or it may be that cocaine control programs affect the prices of other substances and that those price changes in turn affect cocaine use through the cross-elasticity of demand for cocaine with respect to the price of the other substances.

Regardless, the committee appears to be taking the position that cost-effectiveness models of cocaine control programs cannot yield usable policy insights unless they include interactions with other drugs.[11] If so, there is little prospect of such endeavors informing policymakers in the near or medium term. As the committee notes, it is not even clear whether cocaine and other substances are complements or substitutes. The answer may be different for different substances, time horizons, and subpopulations. It will be many years before these issues are satisfactorily resolved, if they ever are. Our opinion, however, is that the first-order effects of cocaine control programs on cocaine use do not occur through these indirect, multiple-drug interactions.

## EVALUATING THE RELIABILITY OF THE MODEL

The committee is correct in asserting that the *CC* model has not been validated, but none of the methods the committee lists as "common" (p. 27) would have been of use in this case. As pointed out above, good data for validation are lacking.[12]

The committee says it

> conscientiously tried to focus on substantive issues that might arguably change the qualitative findings reported. . . . [P]lausible changes to the RAND assumptions about the effectiveness of treatment programs and the shapes of the demand and average cost curves might well modify or possibly even negate the study's find-

ings. Hence, the committee concludes that the findings lack sufficient persuasiveness to be used as a basis for policy formation
[p. 27].

As shown above, most of the changes identified by the committee
turn out not to affect in any substantial way the study's findings concerning the relative cost-effectiveness of the four programs. Of the issues raised, only two threaten *CC*'s basic cost-effectiveness conclusion:  the assumption about treatment programs' effectiveness
parameters and the use of an additive model of price transmission.

Of these two potential problems, the first is easily solvable by rerun-
ning the *CC* model with updated treatment parameter values to pro-
duce revised cost-effectiveness results. Thus, to whatever extent the
committee's criticism regarding *CC*'s interpretation of the treatment
effectiveness literature is valid, it is only a criticism of the *CC* study's
specific cost-effectiveness findings, and does not challenge the
model itself or its utility as a tool to support policy formation.

In contrast, modifying the model to consider multiplicative price
transmission is not trivial because the extent to which the "hybrid"
looks additive or multiplicative presumably varies by market level
within the United States.  Thus, the model should be extended to
distinguish among the five or six distribution levels.

But even granting the need to explore other treatment parameter
values and test a multiplicative price transmission model, does that
mean that the findings should not be used for policy formation?
What it does mean is that there is some nonzero probability that
some of the conclusions, such as domestic enforcement's being
more cost-effective than source country control, are wrong.  What
would be the implications of insisting on zero or negligible probability of error in decision aids before acting on them?  Broad application
of this rule would eliminate consideration of macroeconomic models
in formulating fiscal policy or of climatological models in devising
energy policy, since such models are notoriously unreliable.  Models
are applied to help in understanding complex systems because they
are among the few tools that can do so.  But the behavior of complex
systems is inherently difficult to predict, so findings of complex-
system models cannot be accepted with complete confidence.  They
can be accepted, however, with more confidence than assertions

based on no model; the latter are the only alternative if fear of error is going to drive us to demand that models be improved to some arbitrary and immeasurable confidence level before their output can be accepted as a basis for policy formation.

Furthermore, *CC*'s policy-relevant conclusions are not restricted to a treatment-versus-enforcement formulation that is sensitive to the two potential problems mentioned above. The following two conclusions recognize those problems and surely meet any reasonable "persuasiveness" standard:

- A cocaine treatment program with the assumed characteristics (something like $2,000 per admission, with one in eight admissions leading to long-term cessation or substantial reduction in consumption) is a cost-effective way to reduce cocaine use. That is, programs with relapse rates of 60 percent or even 80 percent can be cost-effective. That is a powerful statement given the tendency for nonexperts to think of 60–80 percent relapse rates as incontrovertible evidence of the failure of treatment. And it has important implications for policy and practice; for example, it suggests that evaluations of treatment programs should not rely solely on abstinence rates at follow-up but should also measure in-treatment consumption drops.

- Interdiction and source country control interventions using the technology and tactics of 1992 have limited capacity to reduce cocaine use by driving up equilibrium prices in the long run unless the multiplicative model of price transmission holds. Again, that is a powerful statement, and, when briefed, it often generates fruitful discussion about the distinction between short-term price spikes and increases in equilibrium prices and about the issue of transmission of price increases across market levels.

Furthermore, *CC* generated many important insights that bear on policy which were not challenged or even discussed by the NRC report critique, including these:

- Relative cost-effectiveness changes as one changes objectives (*CC* Chapter Five).

- A small number of users is responsible for most of the use, so it is important to distinguish between light and heavy users.

- As implied above, in-treatment effects can be important.

- Programs can differ grossly in the timing of their impact on consumption (*CC* Figure 3.9 and elsewhere).

- The costs of control can and ought to be compared with the costs of use or abuse.

- The key sources of uncertainty can be identified and, if used to guide research, should lead to more-robust policy recommendations.

## NOTES

[1] For our purposes, economic rent may be understood as profit exceeding the normal return on use of the factors employed in production.

[2] It might be assumed that rents are realized principally by source country producers, but the assumption of rents across all levels maximizes their potential effect on the supply curve.

[3] Supply curves typically slope upward; that is, it takes higher prices to induce producers to supply additional quantities, because producers use the most efficient inputs (land, labor, capital) first, and additional production must thus be more costly. As explained in *CC*, the cocaine market likely differs in that this diminishing-returns effect is offset by the large fixed cost imposed by enforcement, assuming enforcement resources do not vary with production level. In that event, greater quantities of production mean lower per-unit costs and thus, in a competitive market, lower prices and a downward-sloping supply curve. This industrywide external economies-of-scale exception to the usual case of an upward-sloping supply curve has long been recognized in principle (e.g., Samuelson, 1973), but in practice it arises only with exceptional markets, such as the cocaine market.

[4] For this reason, although subsequent RAND cost-effectiveness work generalized the models to allow for convex conventional production costs (Caulkins et al., 1997), this feature was not used.

[5] This was done by changing the formula in cell L263 of the model spreadsheet from

SoProduct*(SoInputPrice+SoRefK*(SoSeizures/SoRefSeize)^h)

to

SoProduct*(SoInputPrice+((SoProduct/SoRefG)^(dd–1))*SoRefK*
(SoSeizures/SoRefSeize)^h),

changing the formula in cell L280 from

SoNetCost + TrProduct*TrRefK*(TrSeizures/TrRefSeize)^h

to

SoNetCost+TrProduct*((TrProduct/TrRefG)^(dd–1))*TrRefK*
(TrSeizures/TrRefSeize)^h,

and changing the formula in cell L297 from

TrNetCost + DoProduct*DoRefK*(DoSeizures/DoRefSeize)^h

to

TrNetCost+DoProduct*((DoProduct/DoRefG)^(dd–1))*DoRefK*
(DoSeizures/DoRefSeize)^h,

where *dd* is a (new) parameter governing the convexity. It is called *dd* here and not *d* (as in the NRC report) because there is already a parameter *d* in the *CC* model. We used one value of *dd* for all three production levels to follow the model in the appendix of the NRC report. The latter collapsed the three market levels into one and thus had a single parameter governing the convexity of production cost. Obviously it would be trivial to experiment with different values for different levels.

The parameter was entered in cell L87, one of the cells left open for such changes. The (production/base-production)^(*dd* – 1) form is used because the model runs over a 15-year time horizon, production in the base case varies from year to year (slightly), and only base production in 1992 is an easily accessible parameter.

[6]It is unclear why the cost-effectiveness of source country control drops when *dd* increases from 1 to 2. It may be because the model is dynamic, the production level varies over the period modeled, and the processing cost function with *dd* > 1 can be forced to pass through the original cost for only one level of production, i.e., for one year. (That year is the 1992 baseline level.) But that is just a conjecture.

[7]Indeed, the analyses described above (with the exception of making *gg* > 1) took one of us less than two hours to conduct, even though that person had never used the model before.

[8]The cited research was done for RAND, which sponsored some of the early work on the multiplicative model precisely because the *CC* analysis flagged its importance. That work was a significant factor in the multiplicative model's being considered as a serious contender to the additive model in subsequent years.

[9]The quote above may lead some readers to infer that the committee believes *CC* should have considered user sanctions. In fact, the committee explicitly observes earlier in its report (p. 10) that *CC* does not address such sanctions. Unreported side calculations suggested to *CC*'s authors that imprisoning users would be less cost-effective than domestic enforcement against suppliers. Presumably fines, if collected, would be very cost-effective from the taxpayers' perspective. Of course, this is all irrelevant to the cost-effectiveness of enforcement against dealers, which is how *CC* defines "domestic enforcement." There are many potentially helpful interventions other than user sanctions that fell outside *CC*'s scope; these include drug prevention, diversion control programs, weed-and-seed efforts, and currency control regulations.

[10]Cross-price elasticities measure the influence of changes in the price of one product on consumption of others. A change in price of one good (e.g., a rise in the price of bacon) may cause a change in the same direction in the consumption of another good (e.g., a rise in the consumption of sausage); if so, the two goods are termed *substitutes*. Conversely, a change in price in one good (e.g., a rise in the price of eggs) may cause a change in the opposite direction in the consumption of another good (e.g., a drop in the consumption of bacon); if so, the two goods are termed *complements*.

[11]"It is clear that understanding patterns of complementarity and substitution among drugs is essential to understanding the effects of control policies on use" (p. 27).

[12]While a full validation is not feasible, Boyum (1995) performed a quick analysis that is of some interest. As he pointed out, it can be inferred from the *CC* model that each dollar spent on enforcement raises drug prices by three dollars. Separately, it has been estimated that users spent $37.6 billion on cocaine in 1992. It is generally estimated that some 95 percent of the price of cocaine covers the costs enforcement imposes on producers, smugglers, and dealers. As reported in *CC*, $12 billion was spent on law enforcement in 1992. These numbers thus yield the same 3:1 ratio as generated by the model.

## References

Boyum, David (1992), *Reflections on Economic Theory and Drug Enforcement*, Ph.D. dissertation, Harvard University, Cambridge, Mass.

—— (1995), *Costs and Benefits of Drug Treatment and Drug Enforcement: A Review of the CALDATA and RAND Studies*, Office of National Drug Control Policy, Washington, D.C.

Bresnahan, T. (1989), "Empirical Studies of Industries with Market Power," in R. L. Schmalensee and R. D. Willig (eds.), *Handbook of Industrial Organization*, Vol. 2, Elsevier Science B. V., Amsterdam.

Caulkins, Jonathan P. (1994a), *Developing Price Series for Cocaine*, MR-317-DPRC, RAND, Santa Monica, Calif.

—— (1994b), "Evaluating the Effectiveness of Interdiction and Source Country Control," in *Proceedings of Economics of the Narcotics Industry Conference* (November 21–22, 1994), Bureau of Intelligence and Research, U.S. Department of State and the Central Intelligence Agency; also available as RP-410, RAND, Santa Monica, Calif.

—— (1995), *Estimating Elasticities of Demand for Cocaine and Heroin with Data from the Drug Use Forecasting System*, Working Paper Series, H. John Heinz III School of Public Policy and Management, Carnegie Mellon University, Pittsburgh.

—— (1998), "The Cost-Effectiveness of Civil Remedies: The Case of Drug Control Interventions," in Lorraine Green Maserolle and Janice Roehl (eds.), *Crime Prevention Studies*, Vol. 9, pp. 219–237.

Caulkins, Jonathan P., and Peter Reuter (1998), "What Price Data Tell Us About Drug Markets," *Journal of Drug Issues*, Vol. 28, No. 3, pp. 593–612.

Caulkins, Jonathan P., C. Peter Rydell, Susan S. Everingham, James Chiesa, and Shawn Bushway (1999), *An Ounce of Prevention, a Pound of Uncertainty: The Cost-Effectiveness of School-Based Drug Prevention Programs*, MR-923-RWJ, RAND, Santa Monica, Calif.

Caulkins, Jonathan P., C. Peter Rydell, William L. Schwabe, and James Chiesa (1997), *Mandatory Minimum Drug Sentences: Throwing Away the Key or the Taxpayers' Money?* MR-827-DPRC, RAND, Santa Monica, Calif.

Grossman, M., F. J. Chaloupka, and C. C. Brown (1996), *The Demand for Cocaine by Young Adults: A Rational Addiction Approach,* Working Paper No. 5713, National Bureau of Economic Research, Cambridge, Mass.

Hubbard, R. L., et al. (1989), *Drug Abuse Treatment: A National Study of Effectiveness,* University of North Carolina Press, Chapel Hill.

Institute of Medicine, Committee on Opportunities in Drug Abuse Research (1996), *Pathways of Addiction: Opportunities in Drug Abuse Research,* National Academy Press, Washington, D.C.

Kleiman, Mark A.R. (1993), "Enforcement Swamping: A Positive Feedback Mechanism in Rates of Illicit Activity," *Mathematical and Computer Modeling,* Vol. 17, pp. 65–75.

Manski, Charles F., John V. Pepper, and Yonette F. Thomas (1999), *Assessment of Two Cost-Effectiveness Studies on Cocaine Control Policy,* National Research Council, National Academy Press, Washington, D.C.

Reuter, Peter, and Mark A.R. Kleiman (1986), "Risks and Prices: An Economic Analysis of Drug Enforcement," in M. Tonry and N. Morris (eds.), *Crime and Justice: An Annual Review of Research,* Vol. 7, University of Chicago Press, Chicago.

Reuter, P., R. MacCoun, and P. Murphy (1990), *Money from Crime: A Study of the Economics of Drug Dealing in Washington, D.C.,* RAND, Santa Monica, Calif.

Riley, Kevin Jack (1997), *Crack, Powder Cocaine, and Heroin: Drug Purchase and Use Patterns in Six U.S. Cities,* National Institute of Justice, Washington, D.C.

Rocheleau, A. M., and D. Boyum (1994), *Measuring Heroin Availability in Three Cities,* Office of National Drug Control Policy, Washington, D.C.

Rydell, C. Peter, and Susan S. Everingham (1994), *Controlling Cocaine: Supply Versus Demand Programs*, MR-331-ONDCP/A/DPRC, RAND, Santa Monica, Calif.

Samuelson, Paul A. (1973), *Economics, Ninth Edition*, New York: McGraw-Hill Book Company.